ANGER
MANAGEMENT

FOR
TODDLERS

PH. JOHAN GARSON

ISBN: 9798491321711
Imprint: Independently published

Table of Contents

INTRODUCTION

Parents know that children can both show intense feelings and have short attention spans. Although giggling, they will explode into a furious fit of anger a second after. Tantrum among toddlers is a widespread behavior. They are starting to learn that they are different from the people in their environment. Therefore, it implies that they want to stand out as well, express their likes and dislikes and opinions. Similarly, they"re just starting to understand the skills of waiting, sharing, and turn-taking. The toddler is now capable of more but cannot wholly communicate and has no power over their surroundings. Frustration can easily result in rage.

Since toddlers have yet to talk about feelings, they rely heavily on their actions to express their thoughts and moods. They will point at the toy and lead you to it, meaning, "Mummy, I want that one, I need it." When They are drained, exasperated, annoyed, or overburdened, they might hit or kick you: "Get out of here! I need a breather." "I want what you have! "Compared to many areas of development, children display varying degrees of tantrums. The children who are intense and appear to "react big" have a more challenging time regulating their emotions. Big reactors use their actions to convey their feelings better. Toddlers begin to outgrow their temper tantrums, learn to control their language, and acquire composure. Until they reach that point, there are steps to manage the tantrums.

UNDERSTANDING YOUR BABY'S
TANTRUMS

The first year of a new baby"s life is spent with parents getting to know their child"s moods. However, about the age of one, babies become more prone to tantrums, catching even the most attentive parent off guard. In the blink of an eye, a happy baby can go from content to having a full-fledged meltdown. Even if it is challenging, a parent needs to stay calm amid the screams. Irritation is the root cause of the majority of tantrums. It may take some time for toddlers to learn how to express themselves, and the gap between what they want and what they"re trying to say is usually the starting point for a tantrum.

During a tantrum, as a parent, you should first consider whether the tantrum is caused by something else, such as fatigue or hunger. Babies who are overstimulated can act out because they are upset. Getting upset with your toddler would only increase their feelings of distress, not decrease them. They don"t have self-control, and they"re struggling with a lot of unmet needs. Children will not learn to regulate their feelings entirely until they are in their late teens/their early twenties. On the contrary, in reality, Our brains grow that way.

Their upsets are justifiable sometimes. Visualize yourself unable to obtain the things you like. Opening jars is difficult. Everything is an obstacle to your movement in the world.

So the toddlers get upset. For example, your toddler could often get upset for several reasons. You should have several responses. An example of that would be, if you reject anything that they wanted to play with, say to them, "That"s okay. You can play with it later." And then you"d divert their attention to an activity you approve of, like building blocks or some other. When they don"t understand what you are doing, they will begin to figure it out if you remain relaxed, especially if you keep your tone patient and calm. In many ways, kids are like dogs. Distract them from the thing they want, and they"ll forget about it.

It"s likely that they are getting bored with all their colorful toys and are highly interested in other things. This behavior means they are intelligent; they are curious and want to learn! There are many things you can give a baby without investing a lot of money. An example: Take a closed shoebox and fill it with an uncontaminated yogurt container (and nothing else). They"ll find it thrilling to open the box and chuck the toy around. They will be delighted.

You could also take a paper bag and put some objects in there that are safe for them to play with. You just have to gather some exciting things to hand them when they seem bored or want to play with something for adults. Fortunately, until they remove the lid to see what is inside, they"ll have fun doing that regardless of the discoveries. A baby purse is also fun too. Get an old purse without long straps and fill it with things similar to what Mommy"s purses have (except for small items, obviously). Play keys, sunglasses, child"s play cell phone, things that would be okay for the child to put in their mouth. It won"t be long before the child figures it out, but many babies have fun with the purse trick!

The other reason babies will be distressed is that they are just starting to walk. Trying to learn how to walk is just as painful as going to the gym or running five miles for the first time. Once toddlers are walking, they want to go everywhere they couldn"t go before, so they can get pretty worked up about things like not being let in the kitchen. A baby in the kitchen crawling around underfoot isn"t safe. Moments like this are one of the periods they can"t have what they want. It is utterly appropriate for the kid to feel dissatisfaction and rage. You can respond by soothing them while calmly saying no, no. "I know you want that, but Mommy says no" and then offer something else.

When you are trying to cook, and they are all over you, tell them that you understand how they think, but let them have their moment. It wouldn"t take long for the toddler to realize they will not get their way by crying. But they should also know that you aren"t ignoring them. It would help if you often repeated to them. "You"re okay. I understand you"re frustrated, and that"s awesome, but Mommy isn"t going to change her mind. You are not allowed to be present in the kitchen at this time."

Babies love it when their feelings are acknowledged. Recognizing their feelings goes a long way—even before they seem to be speaking in their native languages. Consider making some "fun boxes" to give them in exchange for the forbidden items, and kindly respect their feelings while setting the appropriate boundaries.

HOW TO PREVENT TANTRUMS

The key to avoiding tantrums is to be mindful and anticipate your baby"s needs. Again, this isn"t easy, and if Mom or Dad is tired and frustrated, it"s even more difficult.Wake-up time, lunchtime, nap time, bedtime, and so on should all follow the same routine as far as possible. This predictability gives a sense of security to small children, which is extremely calming.On days when you know the pattern will deviate (grandma and grandpa, despite their best intentions, are notorious disruptors), aim to plan ahead of time.

This predictability may be an extra boost for good behavior or an impromptu nap if a baby seems to be fussy.Of course, there is no foolproof solution for ensuring perfect behavior at all times. You will almost certainly have to deal with a tantrum at some stage. Kids have an uncanny tendency to throw their loudest tantrums in the middle of a grocery store or a nice restaurant.

Another thing to keep in mind is that an older child should not use tantrums or unruly behavior to get what they want. If you give in and buy the toy to stop the crying, you will only escalate the negative actions.If you think your baby"s tantrums are regular and out of control, or if it takes a long time to calm them down, contact your pediatrician to ensure there isn"t a more serious health problem.Furthermore, your attitude will influence how you react. Set attainable goals for your child"s growth. Be vigilant with your baby while they are in a new setting or with new people. Work with your baby because they are learning new things and are easily irritated.

It"s a normal developmental stage for all children, and it won"t last forever (although sometimes it does seem never-ending). You"ll get through the tantrum years just fine if you keep your cool and show your baby that you care for their needs.

WHAT TO THINK ABOUT

Minor inconveniences, such as a car seat trip or a toy out of control, are unimportant to certain children while others see them as disasters worthy of a baby-sized tantrum. Your toddler"s personality strongly influences their reaction. Some babies are content to go with the flow. Others, it seems, are more serious, driven, and spirited, just like yours. Of course, it"s normal for any kid, no matter how laid-back, to become angry or upset when things don"t go their way. (You"d probably lose it if you couldn"t hit what you wanted.) And just because your pint-sized provocateur has a tantrum doesn"t mean they"ll be an angry kid for the rest of their existence. It simply means that you must arm yourself with a few tricks to defuse bad moods, quickly calm your kid, and keep your composure.

Try one of these solutions the next time your toddler throws a tantrum:

Give your irritated baby some words. Even if your 6-month-old isn"t talking yet, you should give voice to their out-of-control emotions. When you ask questions like, "Are you upset because the ball rolled away?" or "You must be upset about sitting in this car seat again," you convey that you understand how they feel while also teaching them words they can use later. Furthermore, describing what is going on will help you relax. When you"re at home, swooping in at the first sign of frustration to bring a new toy or a change of scenery can also help you stop a tantrum. If your baby can"t stand the carseat, add excitement to their captivity by giving them an enticing toy or book, but only while they"re in the car. That way, it will preserve its magical power to distract and soothe them once more (and again).

There are no two children or families alike. Consider any questions you may have to help you adapt. What kinds of situations usually lead your child to act aggressively? What makes you think this is the case? What is your typical reaction when your child behaves aggressively? Do you think this reaction is beneficial to your child? What is the explanation for this?

What to Expect From Birth to Third Year

From the time a child is born till the twelfth month, one of the most daunting aspects of dealing with tantrums is that it can be emotionally and physically exhausting on parents. It's common to be annoyed when your baby yanks on your nose and won"t let go, takes your earrings, pulls your hair, bites when breastfeeding. Babies, on the other hand, have no intention of causing harm or distress to anyone they care for. They are using their senses to discover their surroundings. They learn how the world works by chewing, mouthing, grasping, shaking and dropping, and swatting and then seeing what happens, which is typically a significant reaction.

From the twelfth month to the twenty-fourth month, tantrums (hitting, kicking, biting, etc.) typically peak, because then toddlers have strong emotions but cannot communicate them effectively through words. Toddlers also lack the self-control to resist acting on their feelings. They are only just beginning to develop empathy or the ability to understand how others are feeling. They can"t, however, say, "Mommy, I"m mad because Jeff stole my favorite doll.""But I know he just wants to play with me. So why don"t I get him a new doll to play with?" Your child Would instead hit Jeff over the head with a toy truck.

From the twenty-fourth month to the thirty-sixth month, when toddlers are upset by a distressing situation or difficult emotions like anger or jealousy, aggressive acts like punching a parent are normal. These moments can be particularly difficult for parents because they are hurtful. Parents often presume that as their toddler grow in their thinking skills and become more articulate, they will exercise more self-control. This development stage may be perplexing.Because, while your two-and-a-half-year-old can know what the rule is, they lack the impulse control to stop themselves from doing something they want. In this era, emotions almost always triumph over reasoning abilities.

The bottom line is that when a toddler becomes angry, it means that they are out of control and that they need to be calming down before any teaching or learning can take place. Staying calm yourself is the best solution because it helps your child to do the same.

Signs of Anger In Toddlers

Tantrums are a common way for toddlers to express their rage and frustration. Children under the age of four can have up to nine tantrums a week on average. The majority of children will develop out of these outbursts by the time they start kindergarten. Some of the activities associated with tantrums and anger in 1- and 2-year-olds include:

- Sobbing.
- Screaming.
- Biting.
- Kicking .
- Stomping.

- Pulling or pushing.
- Hitting.
- hurling items.

Toddlers will typically outgrow these angry outbursts as their developmental skills advance. Teaching them effective coping mechanisms for their feelings may also help.

Toddler Tantrum Triggers That Are Common

When a toddler faces a challenge, cannot communicate their desires, or is denied a basic need,they may become irritable. The following are several common causes for angry outbursts or tantrums:

- Being unable to articulate one's desires or feelings.
- Playing with a doll or engaging in a demanding task.
- Being hungry or tired.

•Alterations to the regular and planned daily routine.
•Interacting with a sibling or a different child.
• Not receiving what they want.

Some factors can also make your toddler more prone to rage and tantrums, such as:

• Stresses faced during infancy.
• Temperamental variations.
• The science of genetics.
• The environment.
• Dynamics of the family.
• Parenting strategies.

How to Assist The Toddler in Controlling Anger

Human beings of all ages DO NOT weep for no reason. It"s just that those causes can be invisible to you and me and may not even be comprehended by a BABY. They are crying because they are experiencing an uncomfortable physical or emotional sensation. Have YOU screamed at the toddler? Is there a lot of yelling and fighting going on in the house? Babies are afraid of indignation and threat signs. I"d suggest that YOU are the one who needs to learn to control your anger.

I"d also recommend that you get some parental advice because you might be scaring the wits out of this tiny kid, which is not something you want to be doing because it causes lasting damage and personality changes in toddlers. They need most LOVE, protection, calmness, motivation, patience, continuity, assurance, a sense of SAFETY, and being touched and kept frequently. I"m saying that their weeping is mainly caused by fear of what they see, hear, and feel around them. Too many children are being desensitized to violence. They have discovered that the best way to fix a problem is to become enraged.

Although those are bad news, there are some positive news: Between the ages of one and three, your child can learn significantly more coping and communication skills. Having communication skills can help to relieve some of the causes of rage. Most children can share, express their feelings, and do more with their fine and gross motor skills by four. Although you can"t turn back the hands of time, there are many techniques you can use to help your toddler handle and reduce the frequency of tantrums.

Violence can be taught, but so can calmness! I"ve included six secrets to help you teach your children more positive, calmer ways to communicate their frustration.They are basic techniques that, when used consistently, can produce results. Teaching them to your children is one of the most important ways to avoid the creation of violent behavior, which plagues far too many children today. Here are six suggestions to get you started.

1.   **Show calmness.**

The best way to teach children how to cope with anger constructively is to lead by example! So, use those stressful moments to teach your child "on-the-spot lessons" about how to relax.As an example, consider the following: Assume you receive a phone call from the auto shop informing you that your car estimate has now doubled. You"re enraged, and your child is standing nearby, intently watching you. Gather all of your calmness and use it as an instant anger management lesson for your child: "I"m so angry right now," you tell your child calmly. "The mechanic just doubled the cost of repairing my car." Then have a soothing solution: "I"m going for a fast walk so I can regain energy." Your kid will follow your example.

2.   **Stop and take a deep breath.**

When our children express their anger at us, it is one of the most challenging aspects of parenting. If you"re not careful, their Tantrums can fuel feelings in you that you had no idea existed. Be cautious: rage is infectious. It"s best to create an early rule in your home: "In this house, we solve problems when we're calm and in charge." The law can then be regularly reinforced.Here"s an example of how you could put it to use. When your child is upset and needs a fast answer, you might say, "I need to take a break. Let"s get back to this later." Then, leave peacefully without responding. One mother told me that her only way out was to lock herself in the toilet. The boy kept kicking and screaming, but she wouldn"t come out until he calmed down. It took a few "locked up moments" for the child to understand she was serious. And the child knew from then on that Mom would only discuss the issue when he was calm and in charge.

3.   Build a vocabulary of emotions.

Many children throw tantrums because they do not know how to convey their frustrations in other ways. Kicking, yelling, cursing, punching, or throwing objects might be the only way they know how to express themselves. Asking this child,"tell me how you feel," is unrealistic because they may not have learned how to communicate their emotions! Develop a feeling word poster with him, saying,"Let"s think of all the words we might use to tell someone we"re furious," then list their suggestions.Angry, annoyed, furious, irritated, ticked off, and incensed are only a few examples. Create a map of them, hang it up, and practice using them regularly. When your child is upset, use the following words so they can apply them in real life: "You seem to be enraged. Do you want to talk about it?" as well as "You seem to be very annoyed. Is it enough for you to walk it off?" Then, during the day, keep adding new emotion terms to the list as new ones pop up in those great "teachable moments."

4. **Make a poster to promote relaxation**.

There are a plethora of techniques for helping children calm down when they first get agitated. Unfortunately, several children have never had the opportunity to consider those other options. As a result, they begin to get into trouble because the only action they are aware of are unacceptable ways to convey their frustration. So, explore with your child more appropriate "replacer" habits. You could make a large poster with a list of them on it. Here are a few suggestions: Walk away, visualize a quiet place, run a loop, listen to music, hit a pillow, shoot baskets, draw pictures, talk to someone, or sing a song. Once the child has selected their"calm down" strategy, encourage them to use it any time they get upset.

5.   Become aware of early warning signs.

Explain to your child that we all have minor warning signs that tell us when we"re about to explode. We should pay attention to them because they will keep us out of trouble. Next, teach your child to identify clear warning signs that suggest they are getting agitated.Such as "I speak louder, my cheeks flush, I clench my hands, my heart pounds, my mouth gets dry, and I breathe faster." When they"re aware of them, begin pointing them out to them if they get irritated. "You seem to be spiraling out of control." as well as "The hands are now clenched into a fist. Do you find yourself being enraged?" The more we teach children to understand early angry warning signs when their frustration is caused, the more they will calm themselves down. It"s also the best time to use anger management techniques. Rage escalates quickly, and waiting until a child is in a "meltdown" to attempt to regain control is usually too late.

6. **Teach anger management techniques.**

"3 + 10" is a powerful technique for calming down children. You might print the formula on large pieces of paper and hang it all over your home. Then instruct the child on how to apply the formula: "Do two things as soon as you notice your body giving you a warning sign that you"re losing control. Take three long, slow breaths from your tummy first." (Exemplify this for your child.) Show them how to take a deep breath, then instruct them to believe they are on an escalator.

Start at the bottom step and slowly ride up the escalator as you take a break. Keep on! Travel down the escalator slowly, releasing your breath gradually at the same time). "That takes us to three. Count slowly to ten in your head. That brings the total to ten. When you add them all up, it equals 3 + 10, and it makes you relax."

One easy way to explain our breath"s incredible power is to equate it to a remote control for our body and brain. When your child is upset or irritated, their sympathetic nervous system kicks in, causing them to breathe quickly and shallowly. Deep breathing strengthens the child's vagus nerve, which activates the parasympathetic nervous system, helping to relax and regulate a child"s rage and anxiety. Taking positive qualities breaths is one of the easiest ways for kids to relax.

I've learned that having three "go-to" breathing strategies in your arsenal for kids to choose from gives them some power without exhausting them (or you!).There are countless innovative and concrete ways to make deep breathing creative and concrete for an angry kid, but here are a few of my favorites:

- Extinguishing birthday candles. Put all ten fingers up and ask them to blow out the candles as slowly as possible.
- Breathe when drawing your hand.
Keep up one hand, inhaling as you trace upward and slowly exhaling as you move down the finger.
- Elsa Breathing. Take the deepest and longest breath you can through your nose and slowly blow it out of your mouth to make an incredible ice sculpture!
- Rainbow Breathing. Begin at the bottom of the red arch and inhale as they climb the rainbow, exhaling as they descend, adding as many colors as they want.

•Dandelion breathing. Inhale the dandelion fragrance and exhale slowly through the mouth, blowing the seeds and making a wish.

•Figure 8 breathing. Draw a figure eight in the air or on a surface and breathe in on one side and out on the other, pausing in the center.

It is challenging to teach children a new way to deal with their anger constructively, particularly if they have only practiced violent coping techniques. Learning new habits requires at least 21 days of repetition. So here"s my suggestion: Choose one method that your child needs for success and focus on it for a few minutes every day for at least 21 days! Your child"s likelihood of learning the new skill is even higher because they have been practicing the same technique repeatedly, which is how you learn every new skill. It"s also the most powerful way to halt the tide of violence and help your children live more successful, peaceful lives.

Some might be more effective than others for your infant. And interventions that worked for another child or parent may not work for you. Furthermore, strategies that worked during a previous tantrum may not work in the future. When your child is having a tantrum, the first thing you can do is make sure they are not in danger of harming themselves or anyone. During a tantrum, children often lose control of their bodies.

If you're at home, you may want to move them to a quieter place to have their tantrum, such as their bedroom, or to a quiet area away from lots of foot traffic if you"re out. Then imagine what could go wrong. Rule out hunger, nappy changes, and exhaustion. It might be a case of behavioral crying, or they may want to be picked up. Maybe they"re not getting enough stimulation, or they"re getting too much. Perhaps they want to go outside, which would be beneficial. They may be suffering from gas or colic. Concentrate on narrowing down your options. I know it"s tedious and thankless.Take some time for yourself. Take a peaceful shower. Once your child is okay, here are some techniques for dealing with a tantrum in a toddler:

•Ignore the action and encourage your child to finish his or her tantrum. It can be challenging if you"re out in public or trying to drive. If you"re driving, consider waiting if it"s possible to do so before the tantrum is over. If you"re in public, remind yourself that tantrums are natural and that allowing your child to show their feelings is the best thing you can do for them at the time.

•Use a book or a toy to divert your child"s attention. It works best if you can shift your child"s attention just before the tantrum starts. This strategy will not work if they are having a full-fledged tantrum.If your toddler is older than 2, change their position or put them in a quiet time-out. Taking away stimulation will also help your child relax.

•Keep your child until he or she calms down. Depending on the tantrum"s nature, this could be better done by sitting on the floor and wrapping your arms around yourself. You won"t risk dropping them if they thrash out of your control.

•Get down to your child"s level and communicate with them in a quiet, calm voice while maintaining eye contact.

•Set boundaries by addressing the situation with your toddler. You may have to wait until the tantrum is done. Setting boundaries could be more effective for older toddlers.

•Bring some fun to the situation, but never to the detriment of your kids. Make a funny face or voice, or do something else you know your child loves.

•Interact with your child to affirm their emotions and assist them in expressing them. Let them know you understand if they"re upset or disappointed and that it"s okay to feel that way.

•It"s also necessary to avoid the temptation to punish your irate toddler. It can cause your toddler to become more violent, as well as cause more anger.

At this developmental stage, your toddler"s tantrums are one of the only ways for them to express their emotions. Allowing your child to express their feelings will help them better understand and regulate their emotions as they grow.

HOW TO MAKE YOUR TODDLER FEEL LESS ANGRY

One of the most important roles you have as a parent is to help your toddler understand and express their feelings in acceptable, non-aggressive ways. This is not a simple task. It takes a long time and a lot of patience. However, with your encouragement and guidance, your child will learn to control their powerful emotions and reactions over the coming months and years. Most children react well to the three-step model below.

Step 1: Observe and Learn

Thinking about the following questions will help you recognize trends and evaluate the root cause of your child"s actions. You will use this knowledge to assess the best course of action to take.

What"s going on in your child"s life? Where is the behavior taking place? Home? Child care?Shopping mall?Grandma"s place? Is it happening in all or most of your child"s settings? If it only occurs in one location, it is probably the environment (i.e., too crowded, light, overwhelming, etc.) causing the behavior. Is the action targeted at a single individual or a small group of people? Is the tantrum aimed at times at someone in the child"s immediate vicinity? When is the activity most likely to occur? For instance, just before nap time, when your child is tired? During transitions, such as switching from one activity to another? These forms of stressors are commonly used as causes of violent behavior.

What happened immediately preceding your child"s challenging behavior? For example, had you just announced that it was time to put the game down and get in the car? Had another child just snatched a toy from their grasp? Is there a recent change in their world that makes them feel upset, out of control, sad, or less safe and secure in general? Switching rooms at child care, moving homes, a new baby, or the death of a pet can make your child feel insecure and, as a result, less able to control their impulses.

Some critical factors to remember include:

Developmental Stage: Is your child"s behavior normal for his or her age/stage? For example, while some hitting and biting are common in toddlers, biting several times a week is cause for concern.

Child"s Temperament: Could your child"s attitude to the world justify any of the behavior? A very intense, responsive child, for example, may feel overwhelmed in environments with a lot of stimuli, such as free playtime at child care. They may bite as a coping mechanism to keep people at bay to defend themselves. When a child is left with a new babysitter, he or she will hit a parent. Fear is sometimes expressed as frustration in young children (as well as many adults) (not to mention many adults.)

Your Temperament and Life Experiences: Do you find this conduct especially difficult? If so, please explain why. Often a parent"s own experience influences their reactions to their child"s behavior, such as having had parents who had stringent rules about how to behave in a restaurant. When faced with their squirmy toddler at the diner, they may have a short "fuse. "Being aware of these similarities allows you to look at and react to your child"s actions more accurately and in ways that are appropriate for their age, developmental stage, and temperament.Ask yourself, How do you deal with your own emotions when your kid behaves aggressively? Are you able to calm down before responding? How successfully do you think you are in assisting your child in dealing with their violent feelings? What is effective? What do you think your child is learning from the way you react to their aggressive behavior?

Step 2: Respond to your child"s actions based on your best understanding of them.

Consider mitigation—plan ahead of time, based on what you know about your kids. For example, if you know they are nervous when meeting new people, you may want to start flipping through the family picture album in the weeks leading up to a big family picnic. So, they can begin identifying extended family members. You may have a pretend picnic with their Aunt and Uncle during playtime. When you arrive at the gathering, propose to your relatives that they not rush in for a big hug but instead wait for the child to warm up first.

Using these techniques does not mean that you are "giving in" to your infant. You are aiding them in coping with what is a very unpleasant situation for them. This teaches the child how to deal with new people in a new environment, such as school. Assist your child in comprehending their emotions and actions. This self-awareness teaches them how to control their feelings.

Strategies for Coping with Tantrums:
Bear in mind that the efficacy of the strategies outlined below can vary depending on your child"s age and stage of development, as well as his or her

temperament. They are not prescriptions but rather, suggestions that can be tailored to the specific needs of your child and family.

Maintain your composure. This is the first and most critical move. Take a few deep breaths. You can also take a minute or two of your own "time out" to relax. Maintaining power increases the likelihood that your child will settle down more quickly. When you become irritated, angry, and disappointed due to your child"s tantrum, it also worsens their anxiety. When they are "losing it," they need you to be their rock.

Recognize your child"s mood or target. Make it clear to your child that you understand what they want to do: "You want to play with water, but you can"t spill the water from your sippy cup on the floor." Alternatively, you could say "you are incredibly enraged. You want to linger longer at the playground, but hitting mommy is not appropriate. Hitting is painful."

To express your message, use words and gestures. Words alone might not be enough to convince your toddler to avoid engaging in inappropriate behavior. Use an authoritative, matter-of-fact (rather than angry or screaming) tone of voice to help your child understand your message. Simultaneously, use a "stop" or "no-no" gesture with your words. You might say, "No hitting, hitting hurts," as you take their hand and hold it tightly but not angrily by their side. Bear in mind that it requires many, many repetitions of hearing the words and acting until the words alone are appropriate.

Provide alternatives. Tell and demonstrate appropriate ways for your child to achieve their goal or channel their energy. If you interfere in your child"s actions but do not have a suitable solution, the unacceptable behavior is more likely to occur. So, if your child enjoys dumping their sippy cup and playing with their drink, take them outside or place them in the bath where they can happily play with liquids. Make a game of throwing softballs into a basket or box for a child who likes hurling objects.

Consider using a distraction. Try a distraction if your child is highly irritated. Try an unexpected reaction that your child is not expecting, similar to asking a child who is yelling angrily to join you in a game. Or simply approach them and give them a bear hug.When your child is upset, recommend that they jump up and down, hit the sofa cushions, tear a paper, cuddle up in a comfortable area for alone time, paint an angry picture, or use another effective tactic. It would help if you taught your child that there are many positive, non-harmful ways to express themselves and that you help them practice these techniques regularly.

Enable your child to take a break. Some children settle down much faster when allowed to be alone in a safe, quiet location. Giving your child a break is not a form of punishment. It is an effective technique for teaching children how to relax and regain control, a necessary life skill. Consider and refer to this safe, quiet room as a "cozy corner." It could contain pillows, stuffed animals, books, and tiny, healthy toys. Allow your child to assist you in designing it. The more they believe they have a say in it, the more likely they are to consider its use. One of three things will occur :

- They'll pass out finally (fall asleep).
- They'll learn how to soothe themselves.
- They'll start living without you in 20 minutes (IF they don't fall asleep first). But you will be able to escape the screams, which will eventually benefit your mental health. No one will take a breather for you if you can't. No baby has ever died as a result of crying.

Six months marks a watershed point in their liberation.They will learn to crawl, start feeding themselves, become more vocal, and so on. It is time to put schedules in order and to love on them. But also allow them "quiet time" in their crib; this tells them that even though you leave, you'll return (always smile when you come back).You don't have to keep them and entertain them all the time; cuddles are lovely, but eventually, you want them to be independent

Step 3: Help your older toddler (2 ½ to 3 years old), who is starting to understand the reasoning and logical thought, in learning from their actions.

Emphasize the implications of your child"s actions: "Mary began to weep when you hit her.""It was painful. She was both depressed and furious.""She no longer wanted to play with you, which made you sad."

Consider what better choice(s) your child might make the next time. "What other options do you have if Mary takes the little truck you"re playing with?" If your child has no ideas (which is very typical), you might recommend some tactics, such as encouraging them to use their words: "That is my truck." "Please return it, and then offer Mary another vehicle."Remind your child that they can still turn to you for assistance.

After you"ve given them a few suggestions, they may be able to come up with some on their own. The willingness to substitute an appropriate action for a non-acceptable action is a critical component of developing self-control. It is also a valuable ability for succeeding in school and life. Bear in mind that the best time for this brainstorming process can vary depending on the kid. Some people can benefit from thinking about the issue immediately after the incident. In contrast, others need more time to cool down and be more open to this phase later.Here are some other ways you may be able to reduce your toddler's anger:

- Maintain as much of a routine as possible.
- Anticipate and plan for possible changes in your toddler"s routine or environment. When plans change at the last minute, or everything does not go as planned, try to maintain a positive attitude. This will assist in modeling the habits you want your toddler to demonstrate.
- Assist your toddler in expressing feelings by vocabulary or coping skills such as stomping.

- When your toddler meets an obstacle, assist them in problem-solving.
- When your child shows good conduct, give him or her positive reinforcement.
- Avoid placing your toddler in an awkward position or offering them too complex toys for their age.
- Avoid violent outbursts by controlling your own feelings.

Expecting your child to be happy all of the time is unrealistic—toddlers, like all humans, experience various emotions. Talk to your child about how they're feeling and help them understand the mixed feelings they're experiencing.

HOLDING TANTRUMS TO THE

BAREST MINIMUM

Unmanaged rage has the power to derail a day, a week, or a life. Giving your child a head start on an emotionally balanced and grounded future entails assisting them in better understanding and controlling their emotions.For most parents, coping with their child's frustration is not at the top of their priority list. Most of us did not get the memo on how to cope with frustration as children.So, it"s no wonder that many parents are at a loss when addressing anger management for children.

Raising an emotionally intelligent child is a journey, not a destination. It is natural to see improvement in your child"s ability to control their emotions one moment and then see it fly out the door the next. With child growth comes natural ups and downs in a child"s ability to self-regulate. The first step in assisting an angry child is understanding as a parent that anger is a natural emotion for your child to display. Your child will need your assistance to understand and handle it properly.

Only by making room for our child"s frustration can we become confident and relaxed in the face of these little people with big emotions and give the message they need to hear. When it comes to anger, it is possible to get out of the passenger seat and into the driver"s seat.When we set a tone of working with frustration rather than fighting it, we will help our child manage it more healthily. If we"ve established this framework, we can help kids explore their rage in more concrete ways. These are the seven most popular anger management activities I advise parents to use with their Toddlers.

Best Anger Management Activities for Children

Where in your body does Tatrum reside?

Discovering how physical an emotion rage is is a critical phase in comprehending it. As adults, we are probably all conscious of the various ways anger expresses itself viscerally for us.When I"m discussing this with kids, I talk about the body"s "rage signals." When your child becomes more in tune with their body"s rage signs and signals, it"s a strong clue that it"s time to change direction. Exploring this with your child is as easy as making them draw an image of their body, then coloring where rage shows up/comes out/lives, and what they think it would look like.Kids sometimes draw heavily on the hands and mouth area of the image, saying,"rage bursts out of my hands and often throws toys!" or "anger yells out of my mouth with a thunderous voice!". It"s fascinating to see how they conceptualize their rage in physical form.

Personify their rage

Our rage is a part of us, but it does not have to rule us. Rage is a strong emotion that can feel daunting and disturbing to children. Externalizing a problem or difficulty that a child is experiencing is a great therapist technique that I often use with children. If your child struggles to manage their anger in healthy ways, giving their anger a name and a visual representation allows them to separate who they are as a person from their anger issues.The individual is not the issue; the issue is the issue. When a child believes they are a troubled child because they often acts out in school or creates trouble at home, it is more challenging to help them make improvements.

Make a clear comment to your child like, "It seems that rage has been causing you a lot of stress lately." "How about we give your rage a name and draw a picture of what you think it might look like?" When the child can see the problem „outside of themselves," they can logically problem-solve, having greater insight into the problem or situation.

Anger'š Tip of the Iceberg

Anger is a complex emotion, and the more your child understands how it works, the better equipped they will be to deal with it. Anger is sometimes used as a shield or a mask for other empathetic emotions.

It is easier to be angry than to be humiliated, embarrassed, or hurt. Our subconscious wants to protect us, so it sends in its defense team. The anger iceberg metaphor is a fantastic visual that depicts this for children and promotes self-awareness.On every given day, they have activities, feelings, and stressors that lie under the surface of what we can see as parents or teachers.They can be prompted to reflect on various emotions and circumstances throughout the day (or week), then write these down beneath the surface of their anger Iceberg.When your child is focused ontheir genuine emotions and stressors, you can help them work through those emotions and solve complex problems.

Create a „trigger tracker.‟

Helping your child explore what situations easily set them off allows them to develop greater self-awareness and eventually be more prepared in the face of frustrating circumstances through problem-solving and preparation.

Take a piece of paper and make some checkboxes along the left side of the page. If your child is younger, you will need to fill in potential anger triggers/buttons/fuses. An older child can be asked to assist in making a list.

Anger scale

This activity connects several significant components of anger management for children. It emphasizes the idea that anger comes in varying degrees and severity.To create an anger scale with your child, you can use a simple box graph shape (shown below) or a simple drawing of an „anger thermometer." Both charts help the child to identify causes for their anger as well as how their facial expressions and features can change as a result of their anger. If you"re using the thermometer concept, put a ten at the top and a one at the bottom, prompting your child to think of places and things that make them angry and mark where they"d fall on the scale. You might be surprised where some things end up!

Methods to Reduce Misbehavior

Be consistent.

The consistency of laws is critical in teaching children to make good decisions. If a child is punished every timethey throw a toy by having it taken away for a few minutes, they will learn not to throw toys. However, as the laws are constantly changing, it is difficult for young children to make sound decisions. If a tantrum doesn"t get your child to stay longer at the park one day, but four more trips down the slide the next, they"ll be confused about which option to choose, "Well, making a fuss worked the other day, so maybe I should try that again."

Stop bargaining.

This is hard. We want our children to feel heard. We want them to see us as open-minded and good listeners. We"d like to be adaptable. However, bargaining over family rules is a dangerous game. A child who can negotiate for additional cookies or a later bedtime will quickly learn that this is a very effective way to obtain these "fringe benefits," and you will soon find yourself negotiating everything. Consistent rules about things like holding hands in a parking lot, sitting in a car seat, or brushing teeth help children feel safe and secure. They realize that their universe has order, logic, and continuity.

Allow them to problem-solve.

Allow your child to solve the problem on his or her own before interfering. Allow your child to figure out a solution before you step in to help, whether it"s finding the right place for the puzzle piece they"re holding or negotiating with a friend about who gets to swing on the swing first. (When they do come to you to fix the issue, you can help them along by making suggestions: Blocks can be so overwhelming! How about trying to add more blocks on the bottom so that your tower doesn"t fall?) You might be shocked at how capable they are at handling conflict and coping with the problems they face.

When your child demonstrates self-control, shower them with praise.

Children are eager to please. When you react positively to their actions, you strengthen them while also increasing their self-esteem. When you were upset, you stomped your feet rather than striking. Outstanding work! Children who feel good about themselves are more likely to be well-behaved. It is crucial to help children experience and comprehend the natural benefits of good conduct.

CHILDREN WITH ADHD AND ANGER MANAGEMENT

Yes, Even a newborn can cry out of rage if they wake up hungry and aren"t fed right away. As all exhausted new parents are aware, babies cry because they need to be fed, held, or changed or because they are tired, sick, or in pain. And some babies simply have a more negative and intense reaction to the outside world. As a result, the baby is irritable and clingy. Actual temper tantrums don"t usually occur until a baby is 12 to 18 months old. Your baby"s angry crying may appear to be a smaller version of one. If your baby is fussy throughout the day but does not need to be fed or have their diaper changed, They may need to let off steam. Some babies cry to relieve tension or burn off excess energy, while others simply need to cry themselves to sleep.

However, toddler anger is not always caused by the reasons listed above; it could be a mental disorder. Yes, it is known as ADHD (attention deficit hyperactivity disorder). It is not uncommon for children with ADHD to become enraged. It"s not always easy to tell because toddlers have trouble paying attention in general. Toddlers are not usually diagnosed with ADHD.But many of their behaviors may cause some parents to wonder whether their child has it or is at risk of developing it.

However, ADHD is more than just typical toddler behavior. According to the National Institutes of Health (NIH), the condition can affect teens and even adults. This is why it is critical to identify ADHD symptoms in early childhood. These children may find it challenging to manage and regulate their emotions. They may also be hypersensitive. Stressful or frustrating situations can quickly erupt into tantrums. Children with ADHD also struggle to pause and think through problems before reacting. According to the NIH, the following are the three most common symptoms of the condition in children over the age of three:

- Inattention.
- Hyperactivity.
- Impulsivity.

These behaviors can also be seen in children who do not have ADHD. Your child will not be diagnosed with the condition unless symptoms persist for more than six months and interfere with their ability to participate in age-appropriate activities. When diagnosing a child under the age of five with ADHD, extreme caution is required, especially if medication is considered. Adiagnosis at this young age is best made by a child psychiatrist or a pediatrician who specializes in behavior and development.Many child psychiatrists will not make a diagnosis until the child has started school because a key criterion for ADHD is symptoms in two or more settings. For example, the child exhibits symptoms at home and school or with a parent and friends or relatives.

Difficulty paying attention

Several behaviors can indicate your child has attention issues, which is a key sign of ADHD. These are examples of school-age children:

•inability to concentrate on a single task
•having difficulty completing tasks before becoming bored

- Difficulty listening as a result of distraction
- difficulties in following instructions and processing information
- It should be noted, however, that these behaviors are not uncommon in toddlers.
  - Fidgeting and squirming

ADHD was previously referred to as attention deficit disorder (ADD) but the medical community now prefers to refer to the condition as ADHD because it frequently includes a component of hyperactivity and impulsivity. This is especially true in preschool-aged children.

Signs of hyperactivity that may lead you to believe your toddler has ADHD include:

- being overly fidgety and squirmy
- being unable to sit still for calm activities such as eating and having books read to them
- talking and making a lot of noise
- running from toy to toy, or being constantly in motion

Impulsivity

Impulsivity is another tell-tale sign of ADHD. The following are symptoms of your child"s impulsive behavior:

- Displaying extreme impatience with others
- Refusing to wait their turn when playing with other children
- Interfering with others" conversations
- Making inappropriate comments
- Having difficulty controlling their emotions
- Being prone to outbursts
- Intruding when others are playing rather than asking to join in first

Again, these behaviors are common in toddlers. They would only be concerning if they were extreme in comparison to those of similarly aged children.Some other possible ADHD warning signs in toddlers aged 3 to 4 years old. Children of this age can be injured by running too fast or failing to follow instructions.Additional ADHD symptoms can include:

- aggressive behavior when playing
- a lack of caution when dealing with strangers
- excessive bravado
- putting oneself or others in danger as a result of fearlessness
- by the age of four, inability to hop on one foot

It can be challenging to watch your child lose control as a parent. While we can"t make the anger go away, we can teach our children how to deal with it better.

Recognize triggers.

Be mindful of what causes your child"s angry outbursts. Is there a time of day when the tantrum seems to be at its peak? Is there something that stands out? Tantrum will occur at the following times:You will find that the period after school is the most difficult because your child can let down their guard and release pent-up emotions.It could be when they are hungry or tired.There may be triggers that set your child off, such as frustration with a task.

Early intervention is required.

As you become more aware of the triggers, you will intervene before the anger erupts. Be a reassuring presence. Rub your child"s back or arm if they react well to physical touch. Encourage them to count to ten while taking a deep breath. Do this with them to help them understand this calming technique.

Take a break.

Time out does not have to be a punitive measure. Time out is an excellent way for a toddler to get away from the stressful situation and relax for a while.Consider taking a time out in this manner.

Choose a time when your child is calm and happy to talk with them about how to use time out. Allow your child to choose a time-out chair away from the household"s hustle and bustle to give them a sense of control. They will now know how to use it when they need it.Praise your child for being able to use time out to calm down and then spend some time discussing what happened. If your child"s anger caused them to destroy and break their crayons, ask them what they could have done differently to express their feelings in a less harmful, more productive way.

Label their feelings

Reflect on your child"s feelings as you notice them becoming frustrated. "That puzzle is challenging to put together! I see it"s causing you some frustration." By doing so, you"ll help your child become more aware of their own emotions.As your child"s awareness grows, you can assist them in labeling their feelings. If you learned from the teacher that your child had a difficult day with peers, spend time talking with them about how they feel. Assist your child in expressing their feelings to you through words.

Provide options.

Giving your child options gives them a sense of power. If you know, your child struggles with transitions like clean-up time, provide them with a choice to help them get through it. "Would you rather clean up the blocks or the race cars first?" Just make sure to keep the number of options to two or three. A child who has too many options can feel overwhelmed or overstimulated.

Check to see if your child is getting enough sleep.

Sleep problems are common in children with ADD/ADHD. When children do not get enough sleep, they become more irritable and moody. They have more difficulty tolerating stress, are more easily irritated, and their ADD/ADHD symptoms worsen throughout the day.

Make a good example of yourself when it comes to anger management.

It is challenging for children with ADD/ADHD to control their own emotions.So, the more you can help your child understand their feelings and become more aware of alternative, more constructive ways to respond, the better. One method is to set a good example. Teach by example, not only by reacting appropriately but also by going about the process, so your child understands.

Read Books together

Go to the library and select books about emotions, especially those related to anger, resentment, rejection, loneliness, sadness, or any other difficult emotion your child frequently experiences. Consult the librarian for suggestions. Read these stories aloud to your child and talk about your feelings. Discuss how the character handles their emotions. What are the characters" reactions? Could they have handled it differently? How would you react if you were in the same situation? Together, the characters solve problems and discuss positive actions they can take.

Spend Quality Time Together

Make it a habit to spend one-on-one time with your child daily. Make this time together as positive, loving, and nurturing as possible. Children with ADD/ADHD frequently have negative experiences. They must understand how much they are valued and loved. You, as a parent, will make a massive difference in your child"s positive self-esteem. Time spent with you is crucial.

WHEN DO YOU SEEK HELP?

Parents frequently inquire, "Should I be concerned about my toddler"s rage?" Consider consulting with your child"s doctor if your toddler has several angry outbursts per day, despite your efforts to manage the behavior, your toddler"s tantrums frequently last for extended periods, you are concerned that they will injure themselves or others during tantrums.

Any aggressive behavior is expected during the early stages of childhood development. However, if a child"s hostility is interfering with their ability to engage positively with others, explore and learn.If you avoid letting your child play with other children or take them to other events because of their violent behavior, it would be better to obtain advice from a child development professional.

If your baby is crying and you think he or she is ill or in pain, seek medical attention right away. However, if the baby is well, is readily consoled, and appears to be well in between their angry weeping jags. Be careful of how you react to their outbursts. If your baby has a challenging disposition, it"s imperative to stay calm or delegate care when you need it. Babies will also sense when someone is becoming tense or impatient, and they may respond by crying more loudly.

When the people around the toddler are happy, they are more likely to calm down. (According to some studies, troublesome babies are more likely to respond to calm, calming parenting than babies with more even temperaments.)

Don"t be worried about "giving in" to your baby"s cries or temper – it"s a good idea to respond to their needs as soon as possible. You won"t be able to change your child"s attitude, so you"ll have to develop innovative ways to calm them down. However, if your baby is constantly upset or suffers from colic, check with your child"s doctor to rule out a medical condition.Certain patterns do require extra consideration when they often occur and persist over time. As an example, consider what happens when a child:

- Appears fearless or reckless, with a "daredevil" attitude toward life. This approach often results in breaking items or engaging in intrusive actions (entering other people's space).
- Cravings high-intensity sensory sensations. Children who need a lot of "contact" to feel focused may receive this sensory feedback negatively (hitting, shoving, pushing, etc.)
- Engages in unprovoked hitting; behaves violently "out of nowhere" or for no apparent cause.

•Shows a preoccupation with violent themesIn pretend play.
•Following a traumatic event or significant life change, the individual starts to behave aggressively.

Anger in toddlers is normal and not cause for concern if it lasts for a brief period, even if it happens regularly. Consult your child"s doctor if the tantrums become more severe, last for longer periods, or appear out of nowhere. You should also see a pediatrician if the tantrums are too physical or endanger other people, including your toddler.The doctor may encourage you to keep track of your child"s angry outbursts or tantrums to determine the underlying cause. They can also explore various methods for calming them down.

If your child"s tantrums are more frequent or severe than usual, the doctor can refer you to a child development specialist or a mental health professional for assistance.

Tantrums are normal in angry toddlers. When your toddler is having a tantrum, try to use parenting techniques that work for them. Maintaining a routine and assisting your child in expressing emotions can help you avoid or reduce some tantrums. You will not, however, be able to prevent them all. Tantrums are a common part of toddler growth. However, finding professional advice and intervening early may help your child handle frustration more effectively in the long run. In the long run, this will support your child at school, at home, and in other settings.

Made in the USA
Las Vegas, NV
08 April 2024

88423179R00046